En Route to Paris 2024:
Deep Dive into the 2024 Paris Olympics: Athletes, Venues, and More

GW00503544

Table of Contents

Chapter 1

INTRODUCTION

As the globe prepares for the largest sports event of the year, all eyes focus on France as it gets set to host the Olympics from 26th July to 11th August 2024. Athletes from throughout the world will gather in Paris to fight for glory, representing their country with pride and passion. The Olympics is a time of excitement, competitiveness, and celebration of human accomplishment, bringing together people from all walks of life to see the ultimate test of physical skill. Whether you're a sports fanatic, a casual spectator, or a first-time participant, this book is your comprehensive reference to everything you need to know about the upcoming Olympics. From the history of the games to the calendar of events, from the top candidates to watch out for to the locations that will host them, this book is a complete reference for anybody wishing to be fully prepared for the spectacle that is the

Olympics. So come along on this adventure with us as we investigate all the intriguing elements of the upcoming Olympics in France. As the globe continues to recover from the worldwide epidemic, the Olympics in France will be a symbol of optimism and perseverance, showing the strength of human willpower and spirit. The event is anticipated to attract a big worldwide audience, with millions of fans tuning in from across the globe to watch their favorite athletes compete on the greatest platform of them all. The Olympics is not only about sports, it's also a time of cultural exchange when people from various countries come together to celebrate their differences and commonalities. The opening and closing ceremonies will be a spectacle in their own right, displaying the rich cultural history of France and its people.

The Olympics is an athletic event that crosses borders and draws people together from all corners of the earth. It is a period when athletes demonstrate their abilities and compete for the honor of representing their nation on the global stage. The next Olympics in France promises to be one of the most thrilling spectacles of its type, with some of the world's top athletes participating in a broad range of sports. From athletics to swimming, from gymnastics to wrestling, there is something for everyone at the Olympics.

The Olympics is not only about winning gold, it is also about motivating the next generation of athletes and encouraging a culture of healthy competition. The event provides a platform for athletes to demonstrate their ability and motivate young people to take up sports and strive for greatness. The Olympics also gives a chance for nations to join together and promote peace and understanding via sports. The event can bring individuals from diverse cultures and backgrounds together, establishing a sense of togetherness and collaboration.

The host city, Paris, is a worldwide center for culture, art, and gastronomy. Visitors to the city can expect to be immersed in a rich and dynamic cultural experience, with a vast choice of museums, galleries, and restaurants to explore. The city is also recognized for its gorgeous architecture and attractions, such as the Eiffel Tower and the Louvre Museum, which are guaranteed to create a lasting impact on tourists.

In addition to the host city, the venues for the Olympics are also anticipated to be world-class. The organizers of the event have spent extensively developing new facilities and updating old ones to ensure that participants have the finest possible setting to compete in. The venues are intended to give a secure and enjoyable experience for competitors, fans, and staff alike, with state-of-the-art technology and amenities.

One of the most thrilling features of the Olympics is the chance to observe some of the world's top athletes compete against one another. The next Olympics in France promises to bring some of the most dramatic events in recent history, with elite athletes from across the globe striving for gold and glory. From Armand Duplantis to Simone Biles, from Katie Ledecky to Naomi Osaka, there are likely to be some remarkable moments and performances during the Olympics.

Another component of the Olympics that is frequently neglected is the economic effect that it might have on the host nation. The Olympics is a big event that draws millions of tourists and earns billions of dollars in income. The event provides employment and fosters economic development, offering a boost to the local economy. It also gives a chance for the host nation to display its tourism and hospitality business, inviting people from all over the globe.

The next Olympics in France promises to be a remarkable event that highlights the finest of human effort and passion. It is a chance for athletes to compete at the greatest level, for nations to come together and promote peace and understanding, and for tourists to have a rich and dynamic cultural experience. Whether you are a sports fan, a cultural adventurer, or just someone searching for a memorable experience, the Olympics in France is not to be missed. So mark your calendars and get ready for the adventure of a lifetime!

Chapter 2

OPENING CEREMONY

As Paris prepares to host the 2024 Olympic Games, the city is working hard to ensure that the event has a lasting good influence on the environment. One of the key aims of the Paris 2024 organizing committee is to build sustainable and eco-friendly games that show the beauty of the city.

The Paris 2024 organizing team has been working relentlessly to produce an amazing experience for athletes and fans alike, and they have a surprise in store for the opening ceremony.

Headed by Tony Estanguet, a three-time Olympic canoeing champion and the President of Paris 2024, the organizers have opted to break with the convention and host the opening ceremony outside of the stadium. Instead, competitors will go along the River Seine, offering fans the option to view the sport from the banks of the river.

This novel idea is predicted to draw as many as 600,000 viewers, making it one of the most heavily attended Olympic opening ceremonies in history. The choice to host the opening ceremony on the river is part of the organizers' attempts to create a unique and memorable event that shows the beauty and charm of Paris, one of the world's most adored cities.

As the countdown to the Games continues, enthusiasm for the opening ceremony is mounting. With the breathtaking background of Paris and the River Seine, this promises to be an opening ceremony that will be remembered for years to come.

One of the most significant projects ongoing is the restoration of the Seine river, which passes through the center of Paris. Swimming in the Seine has been outlawed since 1923 owing to excessive pollution levels, and the river has been infamous for being trash-ridden and unclean.

Yet, the organizers of the Paris 2024 Olympic Games are dedicated to restoring the Seine to its former splendor and organizing many swimming sports in its waters. In preparation for the event, substantial repairs and cleaning are currently happening to guarantee that the river is safe and clean for the competitors and spectators.

Although the restoration of the Seine is a big operation, it is part of a wider effort to produce a more sustainable and ecologically friendly Olympic Games. Paris 2024 intends to leave a good legacy for the city and its citizens long after the event is done.

Notwithstanding the hurdles, the Paris 2024 organizing team is convinced that the Seine will be able to host many Olympic swimming sports, including the triathlon and 10k swimming marathons. By exhibiting the beauty and potential of the Seine river, the 2024 Olympic Games are poised to create a lasting impression on the city of Paris and its citizens.

Chapter 3

VENUES

The 2018 Olympics in France is planned to be a genuinely national event, with contests taking place in three main regions: Paris, Île-de-France, and across France. This will give you a chance for tourists to discover the vast variety of the nation, from its ancient cities to its attractive countryside.

Paris, the capital city of France, is one of the most recognized and popular tourist attractions in the world. It is also the core of the upcoming Olympics, holding many of the important events, including the opening and closing ceremonies. Visitors visiting Paris can expect to be immersed in a rich and dynamic cultural experience, with a vast choice of museums, galleries, and restaurants to explore. The city is also home to some of the world's most iconic monuments, including the Eiffel Tower, the

Louvre Museum, and Notre Dame Cathedral.

The Île-de-France area, which surrounds Paris, is also a key center for the 2018 Olympics. Paris is home to several of the Olympic sites, notably the Stadium de France, which will host the athletics events. The area is noted for its ancient cities and villages, as well as its lovely scenery. Visitors to the Île-de-France may tour the Château of Versailles, the Fontainebleau Forest, and the lovely village of Provins, which is a UNESCO World Heritage site.

In addition to Paris and the Île-de-France area, the Olympics will also take place across France, giving a chance for tourists to see the country's diverse regions and cultures. The cycling events, for example, will take place in the picturesque mountain areas of the French Alps and the Pyrenees, offering a spectacular backdrop for competitors and fans alike. The sailing events will be staged on the Mediterranean coast, in the lovely city of Marseille, while the football activities will take place in other towns around the nation.

The next Olympics in France will give you a chance for tourists to see the vast variety of the nation, from its ancient cities to its attractive countryside. Whether you're a sports fan, a cultural adventurer, or just someone searching for a memorable experience, the Olympics in France is guaranteed to give something to everyone. So be ready to see the numerous areas of France and enjoy the excitement of the Olympics in one of the world's most beautiful nations.

The Paris Regions:

The Grand Palais
The Grand Palais is a historic facility situated in the center of Paris and has been nominated as one of the primary locations

for the 2020 Summer Olympics. The arena is expected to hold various activities, including fencing, taekwondo, and judo.

Built in 1900, the Grand Palais is an architectural wonder that includes an outstanding glass ceiling and elaborate ironwork. The arena has undergone major repairs to guarantee it is ready to welcome the world's greatest athletes in the summer of 2024.

With its prominent position and spectacular style, the Grand Palais is guaranteed to offer a breathtaking background for the Olympic events. Guests can anticipate a memorable experience, as they witness the world's finest athletes compete in one of the most famous and historic settings in Paris.

The Alexandre III Bridge
The Alexandre III Bridge is one of the most famous monuments in Paris and is a must-visit site for anybody visiting the city.

Named after Tsar Alexander III, the bridge was erected in the late 19th century to commemorate the Franco-Russian alliance, which was created in 1891.

The Alexandre III Bridge crosses the Seine River, linking the Champs-Élysées and the Invalides neighborhoods. The bridge is recognized for its magnificent design, which incorporates intricate sculptures, gilded statues, and Art Nouveau-style lights. The bridge is composed of steel and is almost 160 meters long, making it one of the longest bridges in Paris.

The Alexandre III Bridge is a popular site for visitors and residents alike. Tourists may take a leisurely walk over the bridge to see its gorgeous design and take in the wonderful views of the Seine River. The bridge also gives a good vantage point for catching some of Paris's most iconic sights, including the Eiffel Tower and Les Invalides.

In addition to its gorgeous architecture and scenic vistas, the Alexandre III Bridge has played an important part in French history. During World War II, the bridge was a crucial landmark for the French Resistance, and it was fiercely guarded by Nazi soldiers. Today, the bridge serves as a symbol of the ongoing Franco-Russian friendship and is a monument to the beauty and endurance of the city of Paris.

Lena Bridge
Bridge d'Iéna, one of Paris' most renowned bridges, is slated to be turned into a world-class Olympic site for the future 2024 Summer Olympics. The historic bridge, which crosses the Seine River and links the Eiffel Tower with the Trocadéro, will be provided with state-of-the-art overlay facilities to welcome spectators to see road cycling and sports events in genuinely outstanding circumstances. The Bridge d'Iéna has long been acknowledged as one of the most striking sights in Paris, and its

inclusion as an Olympic site is a fitting homage to its majesty and grandeur. The bridge has played an essential part in French history, and its usage as an Olympic site is a monument to its continuing significance.

The overlay facilities proposed for Pont d'Iéna will offer an unsurpassed viewing experience for spectators. The bridge's exceptional position, with its spectacular views of the Eiffel Tower and the Seine River, will offer a memorable background for the Olympic games. In addition to its gorgeous setting and state-of-the-art facilities, Pont d'Iéna's history and cultural importance make it a suitable Olympic site. The bridge's grandeur and beauty are typical of the city of Paris, and its usage as an Olympic site will display the city's rich cultural history to the globe. The redevelopment of Pont d'Iéna into an Olympic site is an exciting milestone for the impending 2024 Summer Olympics. The bridge's beauty, history, and cultural importance make it an excellent place for the world's greatest athletes to compete, and for spectators to see history in the making.

La Concorde

La Concorde, one of the most renowned public venues in Paris, will serve as a breakthrough and historic Olympic site for the 2024 Summer Olympics. Place de la Concorde, situated in the center of the city, will feature urban sports events with a unique idea that mixes contemporary and spectacular sports with a site steeped in history.

In preparation for the games, additional facilities will be erected in Plaza de la Concorde to welcome athletes and spectators alike. The Urban Park at the site will exhibit novel and spectacular sports, such as breaking, which will make its debut at the Games, and basketball 3x3, BMX freestyle, and skateboarding, which are returning after their triumphant debut in the Tokyo Games.

Place de la Concorde has a long history and is steeped in French tradition, with its prominent position and closeness to numerous ancient sites, including the Champs-Élysées and the Tuileries Garden. Its renovation into an Olympic site is a monument to the city's dedication to promoting contemporary sports while embracing its cultural history.

The pioneering notion of holding urban sports in a historic public area is an exciting advance for the Olympics, delivering athletes and fans a unique and memorable experience. The blend of contemporary and traditional components produces a dynamic and vivid ambiance that embodies the spirit of the Olympic events. La Concorde is a perfect site for the urban sports events of the 2024 Summer Olympics, presenting a spectacular background of Parisian tradition and culture. The magnificent facilities and new sports programming will give athletes and spectators a memorable Olympic experience, mixing the thrill of contemporary sports with the majesty and grandeur of French history and culture.

The Invalides

The Invalides, one of the most recognizable structures in Paris, will be built into a world-class Olympic site for the 2024 Summer Olympics. The Esplanade des Invalides, a wide open park in the city's 7th arrondissement, will be the scene of several of the most interesting activities of the games, including archery, athletics, and road cycling.

Situated beside the majestic Hôtel des Invalides, the Esplanade has become a favorite location for Parisians and visitors alike, where they can enjoy different sports, music, and strolling. Its central position in Paris makes it a perfect site for the Olympics, enabling athletes and fans to appreciate the city's history and culture while enjoying high-level sports activities.

The Invalides is not simply a magnificent setting, but it also has a rich history. The Hôtel des Invalides, situated on the site, was originally established as a military hospital and has since become a significant tourist destination, containing numerous museums, notably the Army Museum, which displays a huge collection of military items.

With the inclusion of the Olympic activities, the Invalides will further cement its position in history as a significant cultural institution and a center of world sports. The Esplanade will be turned into a specific location for the games, guaranteeing a unique experience for athletes and fans alike. Its redevelopment into an Olympic site will give a once-in-a-lifetime chance for athletes and fans to appreciate the majesty and grandeur of the Invalides while experiencing the thrill of the games.

The Eiffel Tower Stadium
The Eiffel Tower Stadium is a gorgeous and unique Olympic site that will be erected in the Champ-de-Mars, a picturesque park situated at the foot of the Eiffel Tower in the center of Paris. The stadium is intended to become a temporary outdoor arena in 2024 and will host beach volleyball games.

The design and location of the Eiffel Tower Stadium will give athletes, spectators, and broadcast viewers a magnificent setting between the Eiffel Tower and the Ecole Militaire, presenting a beautiful background of the most recognizable monument in Paris. The setting will be a great blend of sports and culture, with the adrenaline of beach volleyball set against the majesty and grandeur of the Eiffel Tower and the ancient structures of the Ecole Militaire.

The temporary arena will be constructed to give a superb viewing experience for both competitors and spectators, guaranteeing that everyone can enjoy the sports in comfort and elegance. The location of the stadium is perfect for tourists to the city, as it is readily accessible and gives a unique chance to enjoy one of the most beautiful and ancient regions of Paris.

The Eiffel Tower Stadium will be a magnificent demonstration of Paris's capacity to host world-class athletic events while showcasing its rich cultural legacy. The blend of sport, history, and culture will produce a genuinely unique event for players, fans, and broadcast viewers alike. Its position at the foot of the Eiffel Tower and in the center of Paris makes it an excellent venue for staging beach volleyball tournaments during the 2024 Summer Olympics. The stadium will surely be a centerpiece of the Games, delivering a wonderful combination of sports, culture, and history.

Gate de la Chapelle Arena
The Porte de la Chapelle Arena is a brand-new and ecologically friendly multi-sports facility in Paris' 18th arrondissement, planned to host sporting events and entertainment daily from 2023. The arena will become a significant cultural center for the city, harmonizing with the demands of the region and the City of Paris, and is designed to leave a lasting impact beyond the Paris 2024 Games.

The Porte de la Chapelle Arena will be a universally accessible facility that will expand Paris' resources for organizing cultural events. The arena will have been accessible to the public for almost a year before the Games, giving athletes and spectators a well-established and well-loved site for sporting activities and events. In addition, it is the home stadium of Paris

Basketball, the capital's major basketball club. The venue is created with an eco-friendly approach, guaranteeing that it is ecologically responsible and in accordance with the newest requirements for sustainable development. The Porte de la Chapelle Arena has a mid-size capacity of 8,000, making it an appropriate site for staging badminton and rhythmic gymnastics activities during the Paris 2024 Games.

The Porte de la Chapelle Arena's strategic position in Paris' 18th arrondissement allows simple access to the arena for tourists and residents alike. With its state-of-the-art amenities and ecologically friendly architecture, the arena is destined to become a landmark facility for Paris, hosting world-class sporting events and cultural productions for years to come.

The Arena is an exciting addition to Paris' roster of cultural and sports arenas, offering a sustainable and eco-friendly site for the

Paris 2024 Games. Its location and accessibility make it a great candidate for hosting badminton and rhythmic gymnastics competitions, and its state-of-the-art facilities and ecologically conscious design will assure its enduring legacy after the Games.

The Roland Garros Stadium

Yes! The Roland Garros Stadium, commonly known as the French Open Stadium, is one of the biggest sporting arenas situated in Paris. It is named for the French aviator Roland Garros and is principally utilized for the French Open tennis tournament, which is one of the four Grand Slam tournaments in professional tennis.

Roland-Garros Stadium, one of the most renowned tennis arenas in the world, will play a prominent part of the Paris 2024 Games. The stadium has been enlarged and rebuilt multiple times throughout the years to give a world-class athletic experience. The stadium spans an area of 12 hectares and has 18 clay courts. The current renovation plan, which spanned from 2015 to 2021, featured the installation of a retractable roof with a new design for the Philippe-Chatrier court, as well as the building of the Simonne-Mathieu court, a 5,000-seat stadium incorporated within the Jardin des serres d'Auteuil gardens.

At the Paris 2024 Games, Roland-Garros will be a prominent site, holding not only tennis and wheelchair tennis contests but also boxing events. The retractable cover above the Philippe-Chatrier court will guarantee that the tennis tournaments can take place regardless of the weather conditions. With its rich history and sophisticated amenities, Roland-Garros Stadium is ready to deliver an outstanding experience for both competitors and fans alike during the Paris 2024 Games.

Champs de Mars Arena

The Champ-de-Mars Arena, situated in the center of Paris, is a unique and adaptable arena that will be refurbished for the Paris 2024 Olympic Games. With its enormous 10,000 sqm of size, the arena is hosting diverse events from the fields of art, fashion, and sport, making it a cultural magnet in the city.

During the Olympic Games, the Champ-de-Mars Arena will be essential, holding some of the most thrilling and explosive activities, including judo, wrestling, and breaking. With its adaptable architecture and state-of-the-art amenities, the arena will deliver an unparalleled experience for athletes and fans alike. Situated in one of the most renowned neighborhoods of Paris, the Champ-de-Mars Arena will give a spectacular backdrop to the Olympic games, with the Eiffel Tower visible from the site. The arena's central position and simple accessibility will make it a perfect destination for tourists, who will be able to enjoy the games and explore the surrounding region, replete with cultural and historical attractions.

With its combination of contemporary design and traditional architecture, the Champ-de-Mars Arena will be a unique and memorable site for the Olympic Games. It is likely to give a fantastic experience for all those who attend, whether they are sports aficionados or just inquisitive people eager to experience the enchantment of the world's most renowned athletic event.

Parc de Princes
The Parc des Princes is a historic stadium situated in the center of Paris, and it has been a symbol of the city's athletic culture since its creation in 1972. Having a capacity of nearly 47,000 seats, it was formerly the biggest stadium in France, and it has played home to some of the most renowned athletic events in the world. At the 2024 Summer

Olympics in Paris, the Parc des Princes is expected to be one of the primary sites for football events. The stadium has a strong footballing history, having been the home of Paris Saint Germain since the club's establishment in 1970. Throughout the years, it has seen some of the most iconic moments in French football, with the likes of Zlatan Ibrahimovic and Ronaldinho lighting up the field with their abilities.

In addition to its relationship with PSG, the Parc des Princes has also hosted several big international football competitions. It played a crucial part in the 1998 FIFA World Cup, acting as one of the principal sites for the event and hosting numerous important matches, notably the quarterfinal between Italy and France. The stadium was also an important location for the 2016 UEFA European Championship, as it played home to five matches, including the quarterfinal between Wales and Belgium. Yet, the Parc des Princes is not merely an arena for football. Throughout the years, it has also played home to some of the greatest names in music, with French and worldwide performers playing to crowded audiences beneath the lights of the stadium. The likes of Michael Jackson, Madonna, and Beyoncé have all graced the stage at the Parc des Princes, and it has become a vital destination for music aficionados from across the globe. With its rich history and cultural importance, the Parc des Princes is destined to be one of the most thrilling grounds for football during the 2024 Summer Olympics in Paris. Fans from across the globe will assemble at the stadium to see some of the

Hôtel de Ville

The Hôtel de Ville, better known as Paris City Hall, is a famous monument situated in the center of Paris, along the banks of the Seine river. This majestic structure has been the seat of the Parisian municipal administration since 1357 and is rich in history and culture. The area in front of the Hôtel de Ville has also been the venue of numerous notable events throughout the city's history.

In 2024, the Hôtel de Ville and its plaza will take on a new function as the starting place of the iconic long-distance event, the marathon, during the Olympic games. This is a tremendous accolade for the building and the city since the marathon is one of the most renowned and hard events in the games.

Athletes from across the globe will meet at this historic spot to commence on a 42.195 km trek through the streets of Paris, exhibiting the city's breathtaking architecture, rich history, and lively energy. Spectators and spectators will line the streets, cheering on their favorite runners and soaking in the atmosphere of this unique event.

The Hôtel de Ville and its plaza are not only noteworthy for their historical importance and cultural attractions but also their involvement in the 2024 Olympic games. At the starting site of the marathon, they will be at the core of one of the most exciting and difficult events of the games, bringing together athletes and supporters from all over the globe.

Bercy arena
The Bercy Arena, commonly known as the AccorHotels Arena, is one of the most prominent stadiums in Paris and France. With its unusual pyramid-shaped construction, it has been a hallmark of the city's 12th arrondissement since 1984. Newly refurbished from 2014 to 2015, it is a state-of-the-art, modular arena that can adapt to accommodate a broad variety of cultural and athletic events.

At the Paris 2024 Olympic and Paralympic Games, the Bercy Arena will be prominent, holding sports in basketball, artistic gymnastics, and trampoline. With a seating capacity of up to 20,000 people, the arena is well-suited to holding large-scale events, and its contemporary amenities guarantee that athletes and fans alike will have an amazing experience.

The Bercy Arena's reputation as a cultural and sports center in Paris makes it a great candidate for the Paris 2024 Games. Throughout the years, it has held innumerable concerts, musicals, and sporting events, and its characteristic pyramid construction has become a symbol of the city's dynamic cultural scene. For athletes participating in basketball, artistic gymnastics, and trampoline sports at the Paris 2024 Games, the Bercy Arena will provide an appropriate venue for them to demonstrate their abilities and talents on a worldwide scale.

South Paris Arena 1, 4 and 6

Paris Expo, originally known as the Foire de Paris, is an immense and flexible arena situated in the 15th arrondissement of Paris. Since its completion in 1923, it has undergone several additions and modifications to respond to the changing demands of its guests. With its massive 35-hectare expanse and 228,000 square meters of showrooms, Paris Expo is one of the biggest event facilities in Europe.

In 2024, Halls 1, 4, and 6 of the Paris Expo will be devoted to the Olympic and Paralympic Games, including events in volleyball, table tennis, weightlifting, and handball. The venue's size and versatility make it a perfect site for various athletic events, giving adequate room for participants and spectators both.

With its long history of hosting trade fairs and exhibits, Paris Expo is no stranger to enormous audiences. Each year, it draws 7.5

million tourists from all around the globe, making it a genuinely worldwide attraction. Its contemporary facilities and state-of-the-art technology make it a great location for holding significant international events like the Olympic Games.

As a crucial feature of the Paris 2024 Games, Paris Expo will play an essential role in bringing together athletes and fans from all over the globe, creating a lively and unique environment that embraces the spirit of competition and togetherness.

Île-de-France regions

Le Bourget Climbing Centre
Le Bourget Climbing Centre is a new state-of-the-art sports facility that has been created exclusively for Paris 2024. It is situated in the Seine-Saint-Denis region, and it is the only sports facility in the area that has been created to satisfy the unique demands of sport climbing. The venue is

poised to host one of the most exciting new activities in the 2024 Olympic Games, sport climbing!

Sport climbing is an exciting and dynamic activity that needs strength, ability, and agility. It includes climbing up artificial walls that are meant to replicate the natural environment, employing a mix of speed, bouldering, and lead climbing. The Le Bourget Climbing Centre has been constructed to support all of these disciplines, with five climbing walls in total.

The Le Bourget Climbing Centre contains an indoor wall for warming up, as well as four outdoor walls, three of which will be utilized for competitive events: speed, bouldering, and lead climbing combined. The fourth wall will be left aside for warm-ups, and it has a capacity of 6,000 people, with 3,000 seats and 3,000 standing areas. The Le Bourget Climbing Centre is an outstanding facility that has been created to satisfy the highest standards of safety and performance. It is a monument to the dedication of Paris 2024 to supporting and developing new sports, and to the necessity of offering world-class facilities that fulfill the demands of players and spectators alike.

Apart from its world-class sporting facilities, the Île-de-France area is also noted for its rich history, culture, and food. There are numerous prominent tourist spots in the area, including the Palace of Versailles, the Louvre Museum, and the Eiffel Tower. Whether you are visiting the area for the Olympics or other reasons, there is no lack of things to see and do in this dynamic and fascinating section of France.

The North Paris Arena
The North Paris Arena is poised to be one of the most interesting venues for the Paris 2024 Olympics. The Villepinte exposition complex, which is the biggest facility of its type in France, will be renovated into a

state-of-the-art sports stadium to hold competitions of boxing and modern pentathlon during the games. The North Paris Arena will be a modular facility, which means it can be altered to fit a range of different sports and events. With nine rooms at its disposal, the facility will be able to handle enormous audiences and offer an exceptional environment for spectators.

Situated in the middle of Seine-Saint-Denis, the North Paris Arena will be an excellent venue for sports enthusiasts visiting the city for the Olympics. Villepinte is a busy and energetic city with great transit connections to Paris, making it simple for guests to come to the Games. Being one of the biggest stadiums in the nation, the North Paris Arena will play a significant part in the success of the Paris 2024 Olympics. With its sophisticated amenities and diverse architecture, it will be able to hold a broad variety of sports activities, from basketball to gymnastics and more.

Stade de France

Stade de France, the biggest stadium in France, is planned to become the Olympic Stadium during the Paris 2024 Games. Situated in the city of Saint-Denis, just north of Paris, the stadium was erected for the 1998 Football World Cup and has since become a world-renowned site for major athletic events.

Since its opening, Stadium de France has hosted some of the major athletic events in France, including the World Athletics Championships in 2003, the 2007 Rugby World Cup, and the Euro 2016 Football Championship. In the future years, the stadium will continue to play a prominent role in French sports, since it will also host the 2023 Rugby World Cup before the Paris 2024 Olympics.

In addition to its remarkable athletic qualities, Stade de France is also a prominent concert venue, featuring famous French and worldwide performers each year. Its adaptability and expertise make it the right option for the Olympic Stadium, where it will host athletics and rugby sports.

With a capacity of over 80,000 people, Stade de France is one of the biggest stadiums in Europe, giving a genuinely unforgettable experience for both athletes and fans. The stadium is readily accessible by public transit, having a multitude of metro, rail, and bus connections linking it to the city of Paris.

Being the centerpiece of the Paris 2024 Olympics, Stadium de France will play a vital role in creating an outstanding experience for visitors to the Games. Whether you are a sports enthusiast or just seeking to be a part of one of the world's biggest athletic events, Stade de France is guaranteed to create an exciting atmosphere that will remain with you long after the Games have finished

Aquatics center
The Olympic Aquatics Centre is one of the two permanent sports facilities that will be developed for the Paris 2024 Games. Situated in Saint-Denis, directly beside the Stade de France, this state-of-the-art arena is intended to fulfill the demands of both athletes and local people.

Aside from its usage during the Games, the Aquatics Centre will be a useful addition to Seine-Saint-Denis, which now lacks suitable sports facilities. The venue's sustainable design uses bio-sourced materials, making it a low-carbon facility that sets a new bar for ecologically friendly sports facilities.

Having a seating capacity of 15,000, the Aquatics Centre will hold water polo, diving, and artistic swimming events during the Games. The arena will also play a significant role in promoting the French swimming community since it will be utilized to organize important international championships in the future.

The Aquatics Centre's position, only a stone's throw away from the Stade de France, is extremely advantageous for spectators. A footbridge spanning the A1 highway will link the two sites, enabling spectators to quickly transfer between events. As a center for aquatic sports, the Olympic Aquatics Centre is destined to become a treasured feature of the Seine-Saint-Denis region. Its sustainable design and multi-functional character make it a great asset not just to the Paris 2024 Games but to the future of sports in the area.

Yves de manoir stadium

The Yves-du-Manoir Stadium in Colombes, just outside of Paris, is a facility with a long history that will play a crucial part in the Paris 2024 Olympic Games. With the unique distinction of being the only site in France to have hosted the Games twice, viewers will enter a stadium steeped in heritage and sports prowess.

The stadium's history stretches back to the 1924 Olympic Games when it served as the principal site for athletics events and opened to a joyous throng celebrating the achievements of the renowned Finnish distance runner Paavo Nurmi. Throughout the last century, the stadium has hosted almost 250 athletic, rugby, football, and boxing events.

During the Paris 2024 Games, the Yves-du-Manoir Stadium will be refurbished and remodeled to host men's and women's hockey sports. With a seating capacity of

18,000, the stadium will be able to accommodate a significant number of devoted supporters. The stadium's refurbishment will guarantee that it is equipped with the newest facilities and services for players and fans alike. By leveraging the full potential of this existing site, Paris 2024 is proving its commitment to sustainability and ethical use of resources.

With its rich history, the Yves-du-Manoir Stadium is an iconic site that wonderfully represents the spirit of the Olympic Games. As the site for the hockey games, it will once again be at the center of athletic greatness, bringing together players and spectators from across the globe to celebrate the greatest in sports.

Paris La Défense Arena
Paris La Défense Arena is a multi-purpose indoor stadium situated in Nanterre, France. It was initially created for concerts

and exhibitions but will now be turned into an Olympic swimming pool for the Paris 2024 Games. With its innovative design, the Arena can readily adapt to various events, and its outer façade is constructed of 600 dynamic gigantic aluminum and glass scales that give it a distinctive aspect.

The Arena has outstanding proportions and technology, with 28,632 sqm of pitches and courts, a capacity of 40,000 seats, and the world's biggest interactive gigantic screen encompassing 1,400 sqm. The inside of the facility is extremely spectacular, and the grandeur of the stadium will offer an unforgettable experience for fans.

The Paris La Défense Arena is slated to host the swimming and water polo events during the Paris 2024 Olympics. The venue's state-of-the-art amenities, especially the Olympic-sized swimming pool, make it a perfect site for these contests. With a capacity of 17,000 seats, it will offer a beautiful backdrop for these events and is likely to make a lasting impact on athletes and fans alike.

Saint-quentin-en-Yvelines vélodrome
The Saint-Quentin-en-Yvelines Velodrome is a world-class cycling arena situated in Montigny-le-Bretonneux, a suburb of Paris. Completed in 2014, the velodrome is home to the headquarters of the French Cycling Federation and has already held numerous major competitions, including the French track championships in 2014, the World Championships in 2015, and the European Championships in 2016.

With a capacity of 5,000 spectators, the National Velodrome is meant to hold important cycling races and will be a prominent site for the Paris 2024 Olympic and Paralympic Games. The velodrome is equipped with state-of-the-art equipment and a 250-meter wooden track, which will be put to the test by the world's greatest track cyclists during the Games.

In addition to cycling competitions, the facility will also feature a mix of cultural and sports activities throughout the Games, including live music performances and interactive displays representing the history and culture of the Olympic and Paralympic movements. The Saint-Quentin-en-Yvelines Velodrome is a world-class facility that will play a vital role in the success of the Paris 2024 Games.

TheSaint-Quentin-en-Yvelines BMX Stadium

The Saint-Quentin-en-Yvelines BMX Stadium is an amazing arena designed for the Paris 2024 Olympic and Paralympic Games. It is situated inside the National Velodrome in Montigny-le-Bretonneux (78), making it a vital element of the cycling races. The BMX course has been particularly constructed and set out for the Games, with a purpose-built circuit that promises to test even the most expert riders. What makes this stadium distinctive is that it is covered, giving shelter from the elements and guaranteeing that events may take place in any weather situation.

The stadium is available to the public and is suited for all skill levels, making it a useful amenity for communities in the Paris Area and throughout France. It will be utilized primarily for the BMX events during the Games, but it has the potential to hold a broad variety of cycling and other athletic events in the future.

Has a capacity of 3000. Thousands of fans will be able to see the world's greatest BMX riders fighting for Olympic and Paralympic gold. With its spectacular architecture and state-of-the-art amenities, this arena promises to be a centerpiece of the Paris 2024 Games.

Golf National

Golf National is a famous golf venue situated in the scenic Saint-Quentin-en-Yvelines area of France. The 139-hectare complex comprises three unique zones, including a 7-hole beginners course and two championship-level 18-hole courses. The tough championship-level "L'Albatros" course is a real masterpiece, with flawless greens and tricky bunkers that challenge even the most talented players. As a location for the Paris 2024 Olympics, Golf National will display the top golfers in the world as they fight for the gold medal. The course has previously held multiple notable golf tournaments, including the Ryder Cup in 2018, which saw Europe emerge triumphant against the United States. Apart from its world-class golfing facilities, Golf National is also devoted to sustainable practices, including cultural preservation and environmental management. The French Golf Association, which owns and maintains the course, has taken enormous steps to guarantee that Golf National remains a leader in sustainability while delivering an amazing golfing experience for everybody.

Elancourt hill

Elancourt hill, situated in the Paris Area, will be the location for mountain bike sports during the Paris 2024 Olympic Games. At a height of 231 meters, the top of Elancourt hill affords excellent views of the surrounding woodlands and monuments like the Eiffel Tower and La Défense. The organizers have chosen a sustainable strategy to minimize any harmful influence on the area's ecology. 95% of the routes utilized for the mountain bike events are based on existing pathways, and no substantial infrastructure will be developed on the site. This method also assures that the legacy of the Games will benefit the environment, society, and sports. The mountain biking routes have been built by Nick Floros, a famous specialist from South

Africa. The trails will provide a variety of challenges and difficulties for the athletes and will leave a legacy of accessible routes for varied users, from families and youngsters to seasoned riders.

The capacity of the event is 12,300, and the choice of Elancourt hill as the mountain biking site for Paris 2024 will make Saint-Quentin-en-Yvelines a top destination for cycling. Communities that were previously shut off from athletic activities will now have access to a significant heritage, while the area's ecology will be maintained and encouraged.

Château de Versailles
The Château de Versailles, situated in the Yvelines province of France, is a beautiful chateau steeped in history and magnificence. The palace has played a vital part in France's cultural history, and in 2024, it will take on a new function as a location for the Paris Games. The temporary

outdoor arena, which is being created in the center of the Palace's grounds, is a revolutionary spectacle that will stage various equestrian and modern pentathlon sports during the Games. Having a capacity of up to 40,000 people, the arena will be bordered by many stands, allowing superb views of the activities taking place.

The Etoile Royale esplanade, where the arena is being put up, is one of the most prominent spots on the palace's grounds. The outdoor arena will give a chance for tourists and TV viewers a to experience the majesty and beauty of the Château de Versailles in a new and memorable manner. The Palace of Versailles, which was first a hunting lodge and subsequently became the hub of the French monarchy, has drawn millions of tourists throughout the years. The Palace's grounds, which are regarded among the most beautiful in the world, offer a suitable location for the equestrian and modern pentathlon sports during the Paris

Games. With its rich history, spectacular architecture, and gorgeous grounds, the Château de Versailles is a great setting for the Paris Games. The temporary outdoor arena, which is being erected amid the Palace's grounds, is an innovative and exciting addition to the Palace's history and heritage.

The Vaires-sur-Marne Nautical Stadium
The Vaires-sur-Marne Nautical Stadium is a state-of-the-art arena that will play a significant role in the 2024 Paris Games. Situated in Seine-et-Marne (77), it is a unique facility that gives the right atmosphere for the canoe-kayak and rowing sports. With its two white-water courses and a sprint course, the stadium is one of only three places in the world with the appropriate infrastructure to stage these sports at an Olympic and Paralympic level. Following its debut in June 2019, the Vaires-sur-Marne Nautical Stadium has rapidly become a center for water sports in

France. It is home to the national organizations for canoe-kayak and rowing and is meant to attract athletes of all abilities. Yet it is not only for athletes; the stadium is accessible to the public and provides a variety of events that visitors may enjoy all year round.

At the Paris 2024 Games, the Vaires-sur-Marne Nautical Stadium will be in the heart of the action, hosting the canoe sprint and rowing sports. The stadium has a capacity of 24,000, giving it a perfect site for fans to cheer on their favorite athletes. With its contemporary facilities, picturesque setting, and great sports legacy, the Vaires-sur-Marne Nautical Stadium is destined to be a feature of the 2024 Paris Games.

Across France Regions

The Pierre Mauroy Stadium

The Pierre Mauroy Stadium is a multi-purpose stadium situated in the city of Lille, in the Hauts-de-France region of France. The stadium was built in 2012 and has a seating capacity of approximately 50,000, making it one of the biggest stadiums in France. It is named after the previous mayor of Lille, Pierre Mauroy, who was a crucial factor in the development of the stadium. At the upcoming Olympics, the Pierre Mauroy Stadium will host the men's and women's football tournaments, as well as the rugby sevens competition. The stadium boasts a state-of-the-art playing field, contemporary amenities, and a retractable roof that can be raised or closed depending on the weather conditions.

Apart from Olympic activities, the Pierre Mauroy Stadium is also the home stadium of the Lille OSC football club and has held several other athletic events and concerts. The stadium is conveniently accessible by public transit and provides a multitude of services for guests, including restaurants, pubs, and stores.

La Beaujoire Stadium
Stadium de la Beaujoire, situated in Nantes, France, is a historical stadium recognized for hosting the successes of FC Nantes since its creation in 1984. With a capacity of 38,285 people, the Beaujoire remains one of the most recognized stadiums in France, noted for its characteristic curving form.

The stadium had its most comprehensive makeover in 1998 when it was designated as one of the sites for the FIFA World Cup in France. This time, the stadium is scheduled to add a new feat to its record by hosting football events during the 2024 Summer Olympics in Paris. The Beaujoire has a strong history of holding important contests in France, and its selection as an Olympic site is a tribute to its superb facilities and reputation. The stadium is set to be a popular venue for both athletes and fans during the next summer games.

The Lyon Stadium, owned by Olympique Lyonnais football club, is a state-of-the-art multipurpose facility and the third biggest stadium in France, with a capacity of 59,186 people. Its contemporary architecture and ecologically sensitive characteristics make it a distinctive and remarkable site for hosting the Olympic Games in 2024. Constructed to reduce its environmental effect, the Lyon Stadium boasts a 100% renewable energy supply, due to its large solar panels covering the roof. This makes it an excellent example of sustainable infrastructure and green energy methods. In addition to hosting the matches of Olympique Lyonnais, the stadium has been the venue of various high-level events, such as the semi-finals for Euro 2016 and the Europa League final in 2018. It also routinely holds concerts including some of the top worldwide music performers. With its cutting-edge amenities and strong track record, the Lyon Stadium is likely to be a crucial site for the 2016 Olympic Games, and a popular destination for sports fans and music enthusiasts alike.

Bordeaux stadium

The Bordeaux stadium, formally known as the Matmut Atlantique, is a sophisticated sports and entertainment arena situated in Bordeaux, France. It was opened in 2015 and has rapidly become one of the most famous symbols of the city. The stadium has a seating capacity of 42,115 and was designed by the Swiss architectural company Herzog & de Meuron, who is also responsible for creating the Beijing National Stadium, commonly known as the "Bird's Nest."

Bordeaux Stadium is an amazing sports complex situated in the capital city of the Gironde Region, France. Constructed for the

Euro 2016 Football Championship, it is poised to welcome the globe once again in 2024 as one of the primary sports venues for the Summer Olympics. With a capacity of 42,115 people, the stadium is guaranteed to host some of the most entertaining football matches throughout the games. The stadium's unusual architecture, with prominent columns that mirror the adjacent Landes forest, makes it an architectural treasure. In line with its unique design, Bordeaux Stadium was created with sustainability and environmental responsibility in mind, as proven by its 700 square meters of solar panels that assist to power the stadium. Since its establishment, Bordeaux Stadium has been home to the Girondins de Bordeaux, one of France's major football clubs. The stadium has also held a Football League Cup final, the semi-finals of the Top 14 rugby competition twice, and several concerts. Bordeaux Stadium's mix of stunning architecture, sustainability, and state-of-the-art amenities make it a suitable location for the Olympic Games in 2024. The stadium is guaranteed to offer an outstanding experience for players and fans alike.

Geoffroy-Guichard Stadium
Geoffroy-Guichard Stadium, home to the AS Saint-Etienne football club, is a renowned facility that has held significant athletic events in France throughout the years. With its rich history and superb amenities, it is one of the most iconic stadiums in the nation.

Constructed in 1930, the stadium has undergone various restorations and modifications to match current requirements. Its most recent makeover was in preparation for Euro 2016 Football Championship, when it exhibited its amazing facilities to the globe. As one of the sites for football at the impending Paris 2024 Olympics, Geoffroy-Guichard Stadium is ready to welcome the world's greatest players and deliver a spectacular experience for fans. With a capacity of over 42,000, it promises to deliver an electric atmosphere and a breathtaking setting for the beautiful game.

Marseille Stadium

Stade Vélodrome, better known as Marseille Stadium, is planned to host football events during the Paris 2024 Olympics. Home to Olympique de Marseille, this renowned stadium received a comprehensive refurbishment and modernization in 2014, which includes a new stunning roof covering the stadium and its curving stands. Having a seating capacity of nearly 67,000, it is France's second biggest stadium and has played home to all major athletic events held in France including the 1938 and 1998 Football World Cups, the 1984 and 2016 Euro Football Championships, and the 2007 Rugby World Cup.

Nice Stadium

The Nice Stadium, commonly known as the Allianz Riviera, is slated to be a beautiful location for the Olympic football competitions in 2024. With its ultramodern and flexible design, it delivers a unique and memorable experience for fans from across the globe. The stadium's ecologically responsible standards are highlighted by its 7,000 sqm of rooftop solar panels and its system for gathering and recycling rainwater, making it a sustainable and eco-friendly event. The National Sports Museum, situated inside the stadium, is an extra attraction for tourists, showing the history of French sports.

Being a frequent host of high-level tournaments, the Nice Stadium has an established track record of presenting world-class events. It was one of the locations for important matches during the Euro 2016 Football Championship, and its superb facilities guarantee that it is a good choice for the Olympic football tournaments in 2024. Fans will be able to enjoy the Mediterranean environment and the lovely surroundings of Nice while cheering on their favorite teams in this state-of-the-art stadium. In summary, the Nice Stadium is a contemporary and sustainable stadium that is likely to give a memorable experience for football fans during the Olympic games in 2024.

Teahupo'o
Teahupo'o in Tahiti has been hand-picked as one of the stunning locations for surfing at the Paris 2024 Olympics. The wave is believed to be one of the most selective in the world, with gorgeous landscape that will create a spectacular background for the surfing competition. Being one of the newest sports introduced to the Olympic roster, surfing is expected to make an impression at the Games, and Teahupo'o is the ideal site for this remarkable competition. With its breathtaking vistas and difficult waves, the

place has long been recognized by the surfing community, and now it will be displayed on a worldwide platform.

To guarantee that the natural surroundings of the island are safeguarded, the venue will be developed with sustainability in mind. Although the precise capacity of the location is not stated, it will definitely deliver an amazing experience for the surfers and spectators alike. The Teahupo'o wave is guaranteed to offer stunning visuals and set the setting for an excellent surfing competition at the Paris 2024 Olympics.

The decision to designate Teahupo'o as an Olympic location is not without dispute, though. Several local surfers and environmentalists are afraid that the extra attention and development that would come with hosting the Olympics might affect the delicate ecology of the reef and disrupt the traditional way of life in the little community of Teahupo'o. Notwithstanding these issues, there is no doubting the potential advantages of holding the Olympics to Teahupo'o.

Marseille marina

The Marseille Marina is a great site for the sailing sports of the Paris 2024 Olympics. Located in the middle of the city, it provides superb sailing conditions and a world-class site for this famous tournament. Marseille is famous for its competence in arranging boat-related events, making it the appropriate host city for the Olympic sailing contests. The Roucas-Blanc Marina, situated in Marseille, has been particularly modified for the Olympic Games and includes roughly 7,000 sqm of structures and 17,000 sqm of open areas. The basin itself has been rebuilt to match the standards of this renowned competition.

The Marseille Marina is a great venue for sailing competitions owing to its closeness to the sea and the outstanding sailing conditions it provides. The Marina's facilities and infrastructure are of the greatest level, guaranteeing that the sailing contests are staged in a world-class site. With its amazing views of the Mediterranean Sea and the city skyline, the Marseille Marina is a particularly beautiful setting for the Olympic sailing competitions. The renovation of the Marina for the Olympics has made it an even more magnificent location, capable of conducting a competition on the magnitude of the Olympic Games. The Marseille Marina is an extraordinary location for the sailing events of the Paris 2024 Olympics. Marseille's reputation for arranging boat-related events, together with the Marina's gorgeous setting and state-of-the-art facilities, make it an excellent venue for this renowned tournament.

CNTS shooting centre
The CNTS shooting complex in Châteauroux is a state-of-the-art facility that will serve as

a competition site for shooting events at the Paris 2024 Olympic and Paralympic Games. The shooting complex was authorized by the Paris 2024 Board of Directors in July 2022, and it will hold a total of 28 shooting events - 15 Olympic shooting events and 13 Paralympic shooting events. This location, which was opened by the French Shooting Association in 2018, is one of the biggest shooting facilities in Europe. It contains numerous shooting ranges, which makes it capable of holding all shooting events at the Games. Additionally, the shooting facility acquired a new "finals" building in 2022, which means it can now hold international pistol and rifle finals. This facility will hold all the indoor shooting finals at the Paris 2024 Games.

During the Paris 2024 Games, the CNTS shooting facility in Châteauroux will host 340 Olympic competitors and 160 Paralympic athletes who will participate in shooting sports. This state-of-the-art facility is outfitted with cutting-edge technology to guarantee that all athletes may perform at their best. The shooting sports at the Paris 2024 Games will be an amazing demonstration of talent, accuracy, and athleticism, and the CNTS shooting facility in Châteauroux will be a vital location for this fascinating competition.

Chapter 4

SPORTS AND EVENTS

The Paris 2024 summer Olympics is projected to be an entertaining event, comprising 32 different sports and 329 distinct events. This fantastic selection of activities is guaranteed to draw fans of all ages and interests, with something for everyone to enjoy. The sports featured in the Paris 2024 summer Olympics span a broad range of disciplines, ranging from conventional events like athletics and swimming to emerging sports like breaking, skateboarding, and sport climbing. This blend of existing and growing sports illustrates the dynamic character of the Olympics, with organizers continuously attempting to add new activities that reflect the changing interests of athletes and viewers alike.

One of the most interesting new additions to the Paris 2024 summer Olympics is breaking, which is also known as breakdancing. This sport is a sort of street dancing that encompasses a variety of acrobatic and athletic actions, including spins, flips, and freezes. Breaking has been increasing in popularity in recent years, especially among young people, and its participation in the Olympics is a tribute to its rising cultural relevance.

Another new sport in the Paris 2024 summer Olympics is skateboarding, which is an exciting pastime that has been popular in skate parks throughout the globe for decades. Skating includes riding a board and doing a variety of tricks and movements, frequently on ramps, rails, and other obstacles. With its high-flying action and rebellious attitude, skateboarding is guaranteed to be a favorite with enthusiasts of all ages. Sport climbing is another interesting addition to the Paris 2024 summer Olympics, involving a mix of power, technique, and strategy. This sport includes mounting a climbing wall, with participants striving to reach the top as soon as possible. Sport climbing needs a mix of physical and mental power, as well as meticulous preparation and execution.

Lastly, surfing is another new event in the Paris 2024 summer Olympics, reflecting the rising popularity of this pastime throughout the globe. This sport includes surfing waves on a surfboard, with participants rated on their talent, style, and overall performance. With its link to the water and its focus on athleticism and creativity, surfing is a unique addition to the Olympics.

Nevertheless, the diversity of sports featured in the Paris 2024 summer Olympics is outstanding, with something for everyone to enjoy. Whether you're a lover of conventional athletics or developing sports like breaking, skateboarding, and sport climbing, the Olympics promises to be an exciting event that exhibits the absolute best in physical performance and human potential.

In addition to the new and rising sports that are being featured in the Paris 2024 summer Olympics, the Olympics traditionally contains a selection of classic sports that have been a part of the games for many years. These sports include athletics, which comprises track and field activities such as sprinting, leaping, and throwing, as well as swimming, diving, gymnastics, and wrestling. Other popular Olympic sports include basketball, boxing, cycling, rowing, and soccer. The Olympics also contains several team sports, including volleyball, handball, water polo, and field hockey. These sports demand participants to work together to attain a shared objective, with collaboration and communication playing a vital role in success.

Another unique characteristic of the Olympics is participation in sports that are not frequently seen on a worldwide scale. They include sports such as fencing, archery, shooting, and equestrian activities like dressage and show jumping. These sports demonstrate a spectrum of distinct talents and demand accuracy, attention, and devotion.

Chapter 5

ATHLETES

The Paris 2024 Olympics is likely to be a historic event for athletes all over the globe, with substantial modifications to the sports program that are aimed at boosting gender equality and offering more possibilities for athletes to demonstrate their abilities.

One of the most notable changes to the sports program is the addition of the mixed team race walking event, which will see men and women participate in a 35-kilometer route. This event replaces the men's 50-kilometer race walk, marking the first time in the history of the Olympics that men and women will have the same number of events in athletics. This is a big step forward for gender equality in sports and underscores the continuous efforts to build a more inclusive and equitable society.

Another notable alteration to the athletics program is the repechage-round structure, which will be used for all individual track events from 200 to 1500 meters and the hurdles events. This format allows athletes who may have lost out on the chance to proceed to the semifinal level a second opportunity to participate. This move offers a great opportunity for runners to exhibit their perseverance, drive, and ability, and allows them a second chance to establish themselves on the Olympic stage.

With a total of 10,500 participants participating in the Olympics, the event promises to be a display of the world's top athletic ability. From conventional events like athletics and swimming to contemporary sports like breaking, skateboarding, and sport climbing, the Olympics gives a platform for athletes of various disciplines to compete at the greatest level. The variety of athletes participating in the Olympics demonstrates the worldwide appeal of sports and the capacity of athletics to bring people together from all over the globe.

The Paris 2024 Olympics is shaping up to be an amazing event for athletes and spectators alike. With the modifications to the athletics program supporting gender equality and allowing new chances for athletes to shine, the event is a celebration of the power of sports to inspire, unite, and promote good change in the world.

As the Olympics approach, there are countless competitors in the world of sports that fans and viewers alike are looking forward to witnessing participate on the worldwide stage. Here are a few famous athletes to keep an eye on:

Sydney McLaughlin - Track & Field: McLaughlin is a rising star in the world of track and field, recognized for her lightning-fast pace and record-breaking achievements. At the 2021 Tokyo Olympics, McLaughlin made history by breaking the world record in the women's 400m hurdles and capturing home the gold medal. Given her remarkable skill and ferocious competitive attitude, McLaughlin is expected to be a major contender in the forthcoming Paris 2024 Olympics.

Athing Mu - Track & Field: Another track and field athlete to look out for is Athing Mu. The 21-year-old, (then 19) American made headlines at the 2021 Tokyo Olympics when she won gold in the women's 800m and established a new American record in the process. Mu's exceptional speed and stamina make her a deadly opponent in any race, and fans are excited to see how she performs on the international stage in Paris.

Katie Ledecky - Swimming: Ledecky is a household figure in the world of swimming, noted for her domination in distance events and record-breaking achievements. The

26-year-old American has won a total of seven Olympic gold medals and is generally recognized as one of the best swimmers of all time. Fans are thrilled to witness Ledecky race in Paris and see if she can add even more medals to her already remarkable collection.

Katie Grimes - Swimming: Grimes is a rising star in the world of swimming and has already built a name for herself as one of the sport's most promising young competitors. The 17-year-old American made her Olympic debut in the 2021 Tokyo Olympics when she placed fourth in the women's 800m freestyle. Given her innate skill and outstanding work ethic, Grimes is one to watch in Paris and might very well surprise everyone with her performance.

Overall, these athletes are only a handful of the many outstanding and remarkable people slated to participate in the Paris 2024 Olympics. Whether they are seasoned veterans or budding stars, each athlete brings their unique abilities, talents, and stories to the international stage, creating the event a thrilling and uplifting demonstration of human potential and success.

Chapter 6

TICKETING

The Paris 2024 Olympics is gearing up for its ticketing scheme for the games, which will run from July 26 through August 8, 2024. The individual ticketing option was previously offered, after an earlier wave of package sales left many consumers upset with exorbitant pricing.

From now until April 20, interested fans may sign up for a lottery for millions of tickets to Olympic activities. Individuals who are chosen in the lottery will be informed in May and will have the chance to buy individual tickets online.

The original ticketing lottery, which lasted from February to March, enabled customers to acquire bundles of tickets. Yet, many individuals were unable to get lower-cost tickets, prompting irritation among prospective customers.

Paris 2024 organizers revealed last year that there would be a total of 10 million tickets available for the Olympics, with 1 million seats priced at 24 euros ($26) and over 4 million tickets priced at less than 50 euros ($53). A final ticketing session is planned to occur later this year.

Ticket sales are estimated to fund around one-third of the entire cost of holding the Games. With ticket costs anticipated to be more affordable for spectators, the individual ticketing scheme will allow a larger audience the chance to be part of the action at the Paris 2024 Olympics.

If you're wanting to attend the Paris 2024 Olympics, getting tickets might seem like a complicated task. But fear not, as it can be broken down into four easy stages.

The first step is to sign up for the draw. You have until April 20, 2023, to register for the draw. If you've already signed up, be sure to double-check your personal information on your account to verify it's up-to-date.

The second step is to verify the pricing. While waiting to learn about the outcome of the draw, you may plan your purchase by checking the schedule, locations, and various sports sessions. This can help you get an idea of what tickets you want to purchase and how much they cost.

The third step is to check your emails. If you're fortunate enough to get picked, you'll receive an email with a purchasing window beginning from May 9, 2023. Selecting timing will give you access to the single ticket sale for 48 hours. It's vital to monitor your emails often and ensure that you don't miss your purchasing window.

Lastly, the fourth step is to purchase your tickets! If you obtain a buy window, you'll be able to access the single ticket sale and make a purchase in real time. Here is where you'll choose the tickets you wish to buy and finish the transaction.

It's vital to bear in mind that demand for tickets is likely to be strong, so it's better to be prepared and act swiftly when your purchasing window comes up. With these four steps in mind, you'll be well on your way to securing your seat at the Paris 2024 Olympics.

Chapter 7

TRANSPORTATION

Transportation for the Paris 2024 Olympic Games is a major concern for both the organizers and the guests. With an estimated 600,000 spectators attending the different Olympic activities, it is crucial to guarantee that everyone can access the competition locations smoothly and effectively. To handle this problem, Paris 2024 and Île-de-France have decided to work together, with Île-de-France Mobilités being the coordinating authority for all transport in Île-de-France.

Île-de-France Mobilités plays a significant role in allowing 12 million people in the area to go about every day. During the Paris 2024 Games, they will be on standby to supply all public transit for spectators to the sporting sites by greatly extending the transport option. This implies that fans will have access to more trains, buses, and other types of public transit, guaranteeing that they can arrive at the Olympic games on time. In addition to offering public transportation for spectators, the organizing committee has also opted to partner with Île-de-France Mobilités to manage the travel of approved participants by bus and coach. Accredited personnel is those who have been permitted to enter restricted sections of the Olympic venues, including athletes, coaches, and officials. These folks will have a specialized transportation system that will enable them to get to their activities swiftly and effectively.

Additionally, Toyota, the global mobility partner of Paris 2024, will also be assisting with the transportation requirements of the Olympic games. With their knowledge in the automotive business, Toyota will deliver creative solutions to the mobility difficulties that occur during the games. Their engagement in the event will guarantee that the transportation system is not only efficient but also ecologically sustainable.

Transportation will play a major part in guaranteeing the success of the planned Paris 2024 Olympics, with an estimated 600,000 people anticipated to attend the games. To handle such a significant flow of visitors, Paris 2024 and Île-de-France Mobilités have partnered to work together to offer fast and dependable transportation services to and from the competition locations.

Île-de-France Mobilités is the coordinating body for all transport in Île-de-France, the territory around Paris, and allows 12 million people in the region to travel about every day. During the Paris 2024 Games, Île-de-France Mobilités will be on standby to provide all public transit for spectators to the tournament sites by greatly extending the transport offer. This involves designing a transport plan for metro, rail, tram, bus, and the Parisian region's Réseau Express Régional commuter service, in a bid to satisfy Paris 2024's objective for 100% of spectators to be able to reach competition sites by public transport.

In addition to housing spectators, Île-de-France Mobilités will also be responsible for organizing buses and coaches for the 200,000 accredited staff scheduled to be at the Games, in conjunction with global mobility partner Toyota. This will guarantee that certified personnel may quickly and effectively travel to and from the competition locations. This partnership agreement between Paris 2024 and Île-de-France Mobilités is a critical step in ensuring that transportation operates smoothly during the Olympics. With a thorough transport strategy in place and the aid of dependable partners like Toyota, both spectators and authorized staff can rest certain that they will have simple access to the events and that mobility will be a seamless element of their Paris 2024 experience.

Chapter 8

SECURITY

The safety and security of players, officials, and fans are always top priorities at large sports events like the Olympic Games.

With roughly 600,000 people scheduled to attend the 2024 Paris Olympics, the French authorities are leaving no stone left to guarantee the event is safe.

To ensure crowd control, the authorities are preparing to deploy around 35,000 guards, in addition to 3,000 private security officers.

This would allow the authorities to efficiently monitor the crowds and promptly react to any possible difficulties.

To further reinforce their security measures, French officials are also aiming to introduce an AI-assisted crowd management system.

The device is meant to identify disruptions and possible issues more readily, enabling the security services to react fast.

It is worth mentioning that this system will not employ face recognition technology, and privacy issues have been taken into mind in the proposed measure.

One of the most grandiose activities of the Olympics will be the open-air opening ceremony when Olympians will float down the river Seine in front of an audience of 600,000 people.

The AI-assisted crowd management system will be extremely valuable in controlling such a big audience, ensuring that the event goes smoothly and safely.

The draft bill submitted to the cabinet envisions various security measures, such as the deployment of full-body scanners to identify any suspicious goods and hikes in the punishments for hooliganism.

These steps attempt to dissuade any possible threats and safeguard the safety of everyone concerned.

With the memories of the crowd crush and tear gas events during the Champions League final still vivid, the French authorities are anxious to guarantee that similar tragedies are not repeated at the Olympics.

By employing a huge number of guards, installing an AI-assisted crowd management system, and utilizing state-of-the-art security technologies, they seek to provide a safe and secure atmosphere for both players and spectators alike.

It is crucial to remember that the draft bill proposing these security measures has not been approved into law yet.

Yet, these suggestions reflect the French authorities' commitment to guaranteeing a secure and safe environment during the 2024 Paris Olympics.

As the event approaches near, we may anticipate new information and advancements about the security measures that will be put in place.

It is crucial to remember that the draft bill proposing these security measures has not been approved into law yet.

Yet, these suggestions reflect the French authorities' commitment to guaranteeing a secure and safe environment during the 2024 Paris Olympics.

As the event approaches near, we may anticipate new information and advancements about the security measures that will be put in place.

To safeguard the safety of people and tourists, the French government has put in place several security measures, including the heightened police presence, surveillance cameras, and checkpoints at critical places.

With the impending Olympic event in 2024, the French authorities are working towards increasing security measures to protect the safety of athletes, fans, and other participants.

As noted before, the French authorities aim to utilize AI-assisted crowd management technology and recruit thousands of guards and private security people to maintain order and identify any problems.

Security is an essential part of any large event, especially one as prominent as the Olympics.

With the proper precautions in place, Paris can create a safe and secure atmosphere for all those engaged in the event, providing a successful and memorable experience for everyone.

Chapter 9

CULTURAL EXHIBITION

France is a nation with a rich cultural legacy and a long history of artistic, literary, and philosophical accomplishments.

Renowned for its world-famous buildings such as the Eiffel Tower, Notre-Dame Cathedral, and the Louvre Museum, France has captured visitors from all across the globe with its beauty, charm, and elegance.

French culture is famed for its food, fashion, wine, and art, among other things, which have had a great effect on the world's cultural landscape.

Whether you are visiting the streets of Paris, the vineyards of Bordeaux, or the chateaux of the Loire Valley, you will definitely encounter the essence of French culture, which is an intrinsic part of its people's everyday life.

The Olympic Games have long been synonymous with sports brilliance, but the organizers of the Paris 2024 Games are hoping to take things a step further by incorporating a Cultural Olympiad in their plans.

The Cultural Olympiad is a program aiming to investigate the relationships between art and sports and the principles they share, such as excellence, inclusivity, cultural variety, and universalism.

The purpose of the initiative is to bring culture into sporting stadiums and unexpected locations to inspire discussions between sport and culture in all the towns and communities that choose to be part of this trip.

From summer 2022 until September 2024, various huge events will showcase creative projects to highlight the relationship between sport and culture.

The concept is interdisciplinary, and it includes individuals in the cultural and sports realms joining together to produce creative events open to everyone around

France, spanning the four years before, during, and after the Olympic Games.

The program was initially envisioned in 2021 and is being carried out by the Cultural Department of the Organizing Committee for the Olympic and Paralympic Games in partnership with the French Ministry of Culture. The Cultural Olympiad is a one-of-a-kind program that mixes creative practice with sports culture.

Its purpose is to pull culture and sport out of their comfort zone, and it achieves this by holding events in unexpected settings.

For example, activities may take place at sporting arenas or in public squares, bringing together individuals who would not typically come into touch with one another.

The Paris 2024 Cultural Olympiad is a rare chance to commemorate the cultural richness and variety of France.

The initiative is aimed to stimulate discourse, debate, and involvement between the arts and sports communities.

By bringing together artists and athletes, the program strives to promote the concept that creativity and athleticism are not mutually incompatible.

Alternatively, they may be mutually reinforcing, with one supporting and encouraging the other. The curriculum is also meant to be accessible to anyone, regardless of background or ability.

Activities will take hold around France, making it simple for everyone to visit and participate. The program will also comprise a spectrum of other creative genres, including music, dance, drama, and visual art. This will guarantee that there is something for everyone and that individuals from all walks of life may connect with the program in a meaningful manner. The Paris 2024 Cultural Olympiad is a new event that aims to bring together the worlds of art and sport in a genuinely unique and inspirational manner. By fostering the linkages between these two apparently separate professions, the program intends to encourage creativity, promote cultural understanding, and celebrate the variety of France. Whether you are a sports enthusiast, an art lover, or just someone who is interested in investigating the links between these two sectors, the Cultural Olympiad is an event that you will not want to miss.

Chapter 10

SUSTAINABILITY

The 2024 Summer Olympics in Paris are planned to be a showpiece of sustainability and environmental management. The Paris 2024 candidacy was designed with the objective of generating a beneficial effect, in keeping with the guidelines of the IOC's Agenda 2020 and the UN's Sustainable Development Goals. The organizers are building on the City of Paris's proactive environmental policy to make the Olympics a leader in sustainable development.

One of the primary aims of the Paris 2024 project is to build a breathable city by constructing swimming facilities in the River in Paris and the surrounding region and increasing the number of cycling lanes by 2020. This would not only minimize air pollution but also enable 70% of spectators to be within a 30-minute bike ride away from the city's Olympic attractions, making the Games more accessible and ecologically beneficial.

The Paris 2024 Games are dedicated to being ecologically responsible and have approved an eco-responsibility agreement, recognized by the WWF, between the organizers of major athletic events and Paris 2024. This indicates that the French sports sector is capable of reacting to the problems of tomorrow and future generations.

The Olympic and Paralympic Village will be a model of sustainable development, employing 100% bio-based materials, 100% green energy during the Games, and 100% sustainable and approved food sources. In addition, the organizers are aiming for 100% of the Olympic family and spectators to employ sustainable transportation, decreasing the carbon impact of the Games. Approximately 26 hectares of biodiversity will be produced on the Olympic grounds in Seine-Saint-Denis owing to the Games, underlining the organizers' dedication to environmental management.

Additionally, Paris 2024 is aiming to make its sustainable approach of organizing large events repeatable globally and to share it with other international organizers. This will produce a ripple effect, motivating and pushing other organizers to emphasize sustainability and have a beneficial influence on the environment.

The Paris 2024 Summer Olympics are planned to establish a milestone for sustainability and environmental responsibility. The organizers have chosen a proactive approach to environmental stewardship, based on the City of Paris's sustainable development policy to have a positive effect and a breathable city. The Olympics and Paralympics Village will be a model of sustainable development, and the organizers are dedicated to lowering the carbon footprint of the Games and developing biodiversity in the Olympic venues. The Paris 2024 initiative acts as an example to other organizers, proving that sustainable growth can be accomplished in the sports sector, and encouraging others to follow suit.

In conclusion, the next Olympics in France is a significant international athletic event that promises to be entertaining, exhilarating, and unforgettable. With elite athletes from across the globe participating in a range of sports, the games will exhibit the finest of human athleticism, talent, and dedication. Additionally, France, with its rich cultural legacy, geographical beauty, and legendary hospitality, is a perfect host for this important event.

As we have seen in this book, the preparations for the Olympics have been vast and comprehensive, with France leaving no stone unturned to assure the safety and comfort of the athletes, fans, and tourists. From state-of-the-art facilities to efficient transit networks, from world-class hotels to outstanding eating choices, everything is being taken care of to make this a successful and unforgettable event.

The Olympics not only give a platform for athletes to demonstrate their skills, but they also have the capacity to unify people from diverse nations, cultures, and backgrounds. The games are a celebration of the human spirit, collaboration, and kindness, and they serve as a reminder of the unlimited potential of human achievement.

As we look forward to the future Olympics in France, let us remember the principles that these games symbolize, and let us join together to celebrate the greatest of human accomplishments. May the games be a source of inspiration, pleasure, and pride for those who participate and see them, and may they leave a lasting legacy of peace, friendship, and greatness.

Printed in Great Britain
by Amazon

35124454R00066